THE HEXATONIC SOUL SCALE

An Alternative to the Blues Scale
For the Novice Jazz Improvisor

by

Jacob McFadden

TELEMACHUS PRESS

THE HEXATONIC SOUL SCALE: An Alternative to the Blues Scale for the Novice Jazz Improvisor

Copyright © 2019 Jacob McFadden. All rights reserved, including the right to reproduce this book, or portions thereof, in any form. No part of this text may be reproduced, transmitted, downloaded, decompiled, reverse engineered, or stored in or introduced into any information storage and retrieval system, in any form or by any means, whether electronic or mechanical without the express written permission of the author. The scanning, uploading, and distribution of this book via the Internet or via any other means without the permission of the author and publisher is illegal and punishable by law. Please purchase only authorized electronic editions and do not participate in or encourage electronic piracy of copyrighted materials.

The publisher does not have any control over and does not assume any responsibility for author or third-party websites or their content.

Cover designed by Telemachus Press, LLC

Cover art by James Heyworth © 123RF.com

Publishing services by Telemachus Press, LLC
7652 Sawmill Road
Suite 304
Dublin, Ohio 43016
http://www.telemachuspress.com

Visit the author website:
http://www.jacobmcfadden.info

ISBN: 978-1-948046-69-5 (eBook)
ISBN: 978-1-948046-87-9 (Paperback)

MUSIC / Genres & Styles / Jazz

Version 2023.05.16

I like to pay homage to my musical mentors Ron Wilkins, Rick Horn, Jim Oliver, Dr. James Polk and Bahb Civiletti for passing their musical knowledge on to me.

Table of Contents

Introduction to the Hexatonic Soul Scale	i
Hexatonic Soul Scale Treble Clef	1
Hexatonic Soul Scale Bass Clef	13
Circular Breathing	25
A Word on Practicing	27
Comping with Freedom	28
Resources	36
Visit the Author	37

Introduction to the Hexatonic Soul Scale

When musicians traditionally think of a Hexatonic Scale with soul, they often think of the Blues Scale, and they are right because one can't deny that soulful sound that the Blues Scale brings.

Blues Scale

Realize that one of the problems that a novice player can run into is the over use of the Blues Scale in his or her solo. One of my trumpet teachers once told me that the Blues Scale is like salt and pepper, and he was so right because when you sprinkle a little salt and pepper over your food for flavor, the food tastes good. However, when you sprinkle too much, you get the opposite effect which is a stale solo in this case.

Another scale that can be added for improvisation is what I call the Hexatonic Soul Scale (HSS). The reason why I call it the Hexatonic Soul Scale is because it's a scale that can add a soulful flavor to one's improvisation.

Hexatonic Soul Scale

Pentatonic Scale

I didn't include any patterns or licks (except for a few scale degrees) in this book because I feel that it's very important for the novice player to practice getting the hang of creating his or her musical ideas in real time which is what a jazz improviser does. Patterns and licks are very useful for an improviser, but the ability to create one's own musical ideas on the spot is the foundation.

One way to approach this scale is to play the following scale degrees in this order: 5th, 6th, root, b3, root, 6th, root.

When you approach the scale in this order, you will be able to really hear the soulful sound that this scale can bring, and then you can create your solos from there. Of course you can start on any note. This tip is just to give you a jump start.

The audio tracks included with this book are a demonstration of how this scale sounds in an actual playing situation. The Bb Hexatonic Soul Scale is being improvised over Bb7 and Eb7.

Below is the link to hear the Bb HSS being improvised.

https://youtu.be/RxBwqrFDTqU

Here's me playing the F HSS over the first solo section of the tune Moanin' by Bobby Timmons.

https://youtu.be/gZ7_FVVDfkY

Be aware that the HSS can work over a major and minor II-V-I progression as well. Whatever the first chord is of a major II-V-I progression is the HSS you will use. For example, if the first chord is C-7, then you will use the C HSS for that entire II-V-I progression. You do the same for a minor II-V-I progression, but the only difference is that you go up a minor 3rd. For example, if the first chord of a minor II-V-I is A half-diminished, then you would use the C HSS over that entire minor II-V-I progression.

Keep in mind that the HSS can be used over stand-alone major and minor chords as well.

For instance, the C HSS can be used over both a C major and a C minor chord, etc.

I want to bring special attention to major chords and Lydian dominant chords in relation to the HSS because when you go up a major 6th, you can use that HSS too.

Now, let's go back to the major and minor II-V-I progression. Another option that you have is to use the HSS that's up a major 6th on the I chord over an entire major II-V-I progression. For example, if the I chord is A major, then you would use the F# HSS. Another option for a minor II-V-I is to just use the I chord to determine which HSS to use. For example, if the I chord is G-

7, then you would use the G HSS over that entire minor II-V-I progression. You can also use the HSS that's a half step up from the II chord on a minor II-V-I progression.

Since the HSS can work over unaltered dominant 7th chords, realize that the HSS can also work over altered dominant 7th chords. For example, a G HSS can work over a G7#4, G7#5, G7#4#5, G7b9, G7#9, G7#5#9, G7#4#9, G7#5 b9 and G7#4 b9. On unaltered dominant 7th chords you can also use the HSS that's a fifth up.

The HSS can work over melodic minor, half-diminished and fully diminished chords as well. For example, a D HSS can work over a D melodic minor chord, a D half-diminished chord and a D fully diminished chord. You can also use the HSS that's a minor 3rd up over these chords.

Surprisingly, the HSS that's up a major 3rd on a major chord can work over that major chord. For example, the A HSS can work over an F major chord. Also a HSS that's a half step below a major chord can work as well. For example, if the chord is E major, then you will use the Eb HSS. You can also use the HSS a whole step down on a minor chord. For example, an Eb HSS over an F-7 chord.

Understand that you don't have to play all of the notes in the HSS when improvising. You can just improvise on the root, b3, 5th and 6th which is also a half-diminished chord because the 6th becomes the root for the half-diminished chord.

Realize that everything that I mentioned regarding the Hexatonic Soul Scale starting on different scale degrees can also be applied to the Blues Scale.

This concludes my introduction to the Hexatonic Soul Scale.
Happy Practicing ☺

THE HEXATONIC SOUL SCALE

Hexatonic Soul Scale Treble Clef

C Hexatonic Soul Scale

C# Hexatonic Soul Scale

Isabel Da Silva Azevedo © 123RF.com

D Hexatonic Soul Scale

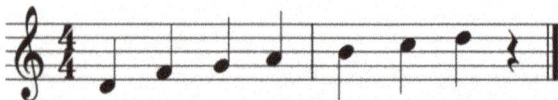

Isabel Da Silva Azevedo © 123RF.com

Eb Hexatonic Soul Scale

Isabel Da Silva Azevedo © 123RF.com

E Hexatonic Soul Scale

F Hexatonic Soul Scale

Zackery Blanton © 123RF.com

F# Hexatonic Soul Scale

Anna Kniazeva © 123RF.com

G Hexatonic Soul Scale

Isabel Da Silva Azevedo © 123RF.com

Ab Hexatonic Soul Scale

Isabel Da Silva Azevedo © 123RF.com

A Hexatonic Soul Scale

ingaclemens © 123RF.com

Bb Hexatonic Soul Scale

Maria Bell © 123RF.com

B Hexatonic Soul Scale

gropgrop © 123RF.com

Hexatonic Soul Scale Bass Clef

C Hexatonic Soul Scale

belchonock © 123RF.com

C# Hexatonic Soul Scale

D Hexatonic Soul Scale

gropgrop © 123RF.com

Eb Hexatonic Soul Scale

alenavlad © 123RF.com

E Hexatonic Soul Scale

mackoflower © 123RF.com

F Hexatonic Soul Scale

F# Hexatonic Soul Scale

Yurly Kirsanov © 123RF.com

G Hexatonic Soul Scale

carloscastilla © 123RF.com

Ab Hexatonic Soul Scale

Isabel Da Silva Azevedo © 123RF.com

A Hexatonic Soul Scale

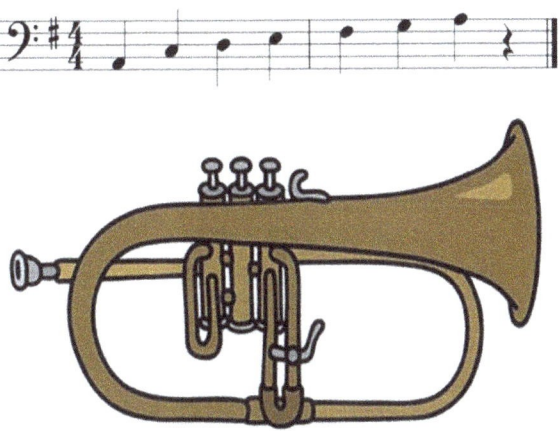

Jana Vostal © 123RF.com

Bb Hexatonic Soul Scale

B Hexatonic Soul Scale

Circular Breathing

When you think of well-known musicians that are great circular breathers, Trombone Shorty and Kenny G come to mind. Circular breathing can be a very challenging skill to master for many musicians, and during my journey, it was downright frustrating. The first two ways that I approached the development of this skill was through the traditional straw in a cup method and the water method where you inflate your cheeks with water, and spit the water out while breathing in through your nose. Both of these methods did not work for me.

The third way that I discovered on how to master circular breathing is through what I call the stopping and starting method. No one taught me this method. I learned it on my own through experimentation, and here are the steps below:

1. Play a comfortable note on your instrument.
2. Stop playing the note while inflating your cheeks out with air.
3. Take a deep breath in through your nose while your cheeks remain inflated with air.
4. Deflate your cheeks by pushing the air through the horn and playing the note again.

Repeat these 4 steps over and over as you work on getting coordinated. What I mean by "getting coordinated" is that you work on getting to the point where you can inflate your cheeks without stopping as you take in air through your nose while you deflate the cheeks by pushing the air through your horn while sustaining the note.

Once you master circular breathing on one note, then move on to mastering circular breathing with multiple notes. For example, work on mastering it on an arpeggio or a chromatic passage, etc.

The stopping and starting method definitely worked for me, and it worked rather quickly. I hope this method works for other musicians as well.

A Word on Practicing

The Jamey Aebersold Play-Alongs that I listed on the resource page of this book are awesome practice tools because they give you the experience of playing with a band. These play-alongs were immensely helpful during my improvisation development, and I still use them today. Understand that these play-alongs are stereo separated which means you can turn off the right or left channel and fill in if you play piano, bass or guitar. Volume 24 is excellent for beginners because it stays in one key for 3-6 minutes, and this length of time will definitely help get the scale under your fingers when you are practicing your improvisation.

Understand that even though this book introduces the Hexatonic Soul Scale, this scale is not the be all and end all. Since the goal of a jazz improviser is to create tasteful solos, definitely practice other scales as well to aid you in the creative process of improvisation.

Comping with Freedom

Playing jazz chords on the piano is quite easy because there are only two positions that you need to worry about which are position 1(p1) and position 2(p2).

Position 1 is voicing the chord 3,5,7,9 and position 2 is voicing the chord 7,9,3,5. For example, a C major 7th chord in position 1 would be voiced E,G,B,D, and in position 2 it would be voiced B,D,E,G. The root is left off because the bass player plays the root.

These positions apply to all chords and the reason why you must play them in these two positions is to keep your hands from jumping around the piano. If you want to voice these as three note chords, just leave off the 9th. Understand that by keeping the 9th in satisfies the voicing for any type of 9th chord that you run into such as a major 9, minor 9, dominant 9 and half-diminished #2 (which is also the #9).

Comping

To comp with freedom, all you will be doing is voicing the chords in your left hand while simultaneously pressing any two notes (you can even use one note if you like) from the scale that matches the chord with your right hand. For example, on a C-7 chord use notes from the C Dorian scale or Aeolian scale. Here's me demonstrating this on the tune Autumn Leaves by Johnny Mercer, and the chord changes are below played in 4/4 time.

| C-7| F7| Bb maj7| Eb maj7| A-7b5 | D7b9 | G-7| G-7 G7#9|
| C-7| F7| Bb maj7| Eb maj7| A-7b5 | D7b9 | G-7| G-7|
| A-7b5 | D7b9 | G-7| G-7| C-7| F7| Bb maj7| Eb maj7| A-7b5 | D7b9
| G-7 C7| F-7 Bb7| Eb7| A-7b5 D7b9 | G-7| G-7|

https://youtu.be/sAevUQS9NKo

Be aware that playing the 4th note on a major scale can cause dissonance. Also be aware that playing 2nd intervals can create dissonance as well; however, use them as you see fit.

Pentatonic scales are used with fourth voicings, but you can use major and minor (Dorian or Aeolian) as well.

The scale that I like to use over dominant 7th b9 and #9 chords is the Phrygian scale because it has the #9 and b9. Plus it's the same scale as the half-diminished when used in the minor II-V-I progression. When playing a four note dominant 7th #9 chord, the fifth also becomes a #5 in p1 and p2 because the chord is derived from the Diminished Whole-Tone scale, but again the Phrygian scale can also be used because it not only has the #9 but the #5 as well.

Voicing the Major II-V-I Progression

|D-7|G7|C maj7|(starting on position 1):
b3,5,b7,9 goes to b7,9,3,6 which goes to 3,5,7,9

|D-7|G7|C maj7|(starting on position 2):
b7,9,b3,5 goes to 3,6,b7,9 which goes to 7,9,3,5

Here's me demonstrating the major II-V-I progression in p1 and p2.

https://youtu.be/VZGv5KEYGBE

https://youtu.be/ZfNDJSrghqg

For three note voicings, the voice leading would look like the following:

|D-7|G7|C maj7|(starting on position 1):
b3,5,b7 goes to b7,3,6 which goes to 3,5,7

|D-7|G7|C maj7|(starting on position 2):
b7,b3,5 goes to 3,6,b7 which goes to 7,3,5

Do realize that you are really playing a dominant 13th (more on this later) for the dominant 7th chord in a major II-V-I progression. Voicing a regular dominant 7th chord would be b7,9,3,5 in p2 and 3,5,b7,9 in p1. Do not worry about the notation so much in this case because it's the ease of playing that counts. When going from the II(D-7) to the V(G7) all you're doing is lowering the b7 of the minor 7th chord down a half step while keeping the other notes the same.

Voicing the Minor II-V-I Progression

The following are the voicings for a minor II-V-I progression using three note chords in p1 and p2:

For example, a |D-7b5|G7b9|C-7| progression would be voiced b7, b3, b5 going to 3, b7, b9 which goes to b7, b3, 5 starting on p2. Starting on p1 it would be b3, b5, b7 going to b7, b9, 3 which goes to b3, 5, b7.

Here's me voicing the minor II-V-I progression in p1 and p2.

https://youtu.be/piIl2I2T1g8

https://youtu.be/bKvhMQadxQI

There are two ways to make four note voicings in the minor II-V- I progression. The first way would be b7, #9, b3, b5 going to 3, 6, b7, b9 which goes to b7, 9, b3, 5 for p2 and b3, b5, b7, #9 going to b7, b9, 3, 6 which goes to b3, 5, b7, 9 for p1.

The second way would be b7, 1, b3, b5 going to 3, 5, b7, b9 which goes to b7, 9, b3, 5 for p2 and b3, b5, b7, 1 going to b7, b9, 3, 5 which goes to b3, 5, b7, 9 for p1. Understand that the dominant #9 can be used in place of the dominant b9.

FULLY DIMINISHED CHORDS

Diminished chords will be voiced the same as half-diminished chords (minor 7th b5 chords) from the previous minor II-V-I section, but now double flat the 7th. To make these four note voicings just add the root. For example, 1, b3, b5, bb7 for p1 and bb7, 1, b3, b5 for p2.

MINOR FOURTH VOICINGS

Minor fourth voicings are basically three note voicings stacked in 4ths that are constructed mainly from the Dorian scale, but the Aeolian scale can also be used. For example, C, F, Bb on a C minor 7th chord. You can even create fourths on the Mixolydian scale.

To create movement, move the chords diatonically up or down when comping. For example, on the C Dorian scale play C, F, Bb going to D, G, C going to Eb, A, D etc. Notice that pressing Eb and A creates an augmented 4th which is totally fine.

Creating this type of movement is only an option. You can still comp by playing three note 4ths in your left hand while simultaneously playing one or two notes from the scale with your right as previously discussed.

Here's an example of me playing 5ths with my left hand (C and G) and creating movement between the fourth voicings G, C, F and A, D, G with my right hand.

https://youtu.be/yqx9PyQfEPs

In this example I went up a half step and added the fourth voicing Bb, Eb, Ab to create tension.

https://youtu.be/10lxGj9WNjI

Keep in mind that you can start on any fourth voicing within the Dorian (or Aeolian) scale. Also to play a major II-V-I in fourths (for example |C-7| F7|Bb maj7|) you would play the voicing F, Bb, Eb going to Eb, A, D going to D, G, C.

Check out the recordings of McCoy Tyner since playing fourths is his signature.

Minor 11th Chords

The b7,9,b3,4 voicing will take care of the minor 11 chord in p2 and the b3,4,b7,9 voicing will take care of the minor 11 chord for p1.

The Major #11, #4 or b5 Chord

Understand that the #11, #4 and b5 are the same note. Voicing this chord in p2 would be 7, 9, 3, b5 and 3, b5, 7, 9 for p1.

Major 6th, Minor 6th and Major 13th Chords

3,5,6 would be a major 6 chord in position 1 and 6,3,5 would be the chord in position 2. To make it a 6/9 chord just add the 9th. To play a 6/9 in fourths, you would play only the 3,6,9. To make all of these minor just lower the 3rd a half step.

Voicing a major 6/9 chord in fourths is the most common way to voice a 6/9 chord and there's no position 2. To add some movement, you can play the voicing 6,9,5 as well. For example, going between 3,6,9 and 6,9,5 when comping.

Understand that the 6th chord is the same as the 13th. To play a major 13, you would play 3,6,7,9 for position 1 and 7,9,3,6 for position 2. I've even heard a great jazz pianist say that voicing the chord this way can be a substitute for a major 6/9 chord depending on what sound you're going for.

Melodic Minor Chords (Minor Major 7th Chords)

To voice this type of chord you would play b3,5,7,9 in position 1 and 7,9,b3,5 in position 2.

SUS Chords (Suspended 4ths)

A sus chord is really a slash chord. For example, a G-7/C (which is another notation for C7 sus) is a rootless G-7 chord that's played simultaneously with a single note C in the bass. Again, when playing with a bass player don't worry about playing the bass note. To make it a C13 sus just add the 9th to the minor 7th chord.

Practicing the II-V-I Progression

The easiest way to practice the II-V-I is to start off on |D-7|G7|C major 7| then go to |C-7| F7|Bb major 7| then go to |Bb-7|Eb7|Ab major 7|, etc. until you go through all twelve keys.

Fingering

Use the following fingering system when voicing the chords with your left hand for p2:

- The thumb is on the 5th
- The index finger is on the 3rd
- The middle finger is on the 9th

- The pinky finger is on the 7th

Use the following fingering system when voicing the chords with your left hand for p1:

- The pinky finger is on the 3rd
- The middle finger is on the 5th
- The index finger is on the 7th
- The thumb is on the 9th

Feel free to use the ring finger to play a b5 in p1.

Compositions

Now that you know how to comp, you also have the tools to create your own compositions as well.

Resources

Jamey Aebersold Vol. 3

Jamey Aebersold Vol. 21

Jamey Aebersold Vol. 24

Scales for Jazz Improvisation by Dan Haerle

Shortcut to Jazz by Bunky Green

Salsa Guidebook: For Piano and Ensemble by Rebeca Mauleon

101 Montunos by Rebeca Mauleon

Salsa & Afro Cuban Montunos for Piano Book by Carlos Campos

Latin Jazz Piano Improvisation: Clave, Comping, and Soloing by Rebecca Cline

The Jazz Piano Book by Mark Levine

Please visit the author at:

www.jacobmcfadden.info

https://www.youtube.com/user/3939jlm

Instagram@jacobmcfadden12

www.ingramcontent.com/pod-product-compliance
Lightning Source LLC
Chambersburg PA
CBHW041320110526
44591CB00021B/2854